I Can Be A
RACE CAR DRIVER

Robin Kerrod & Wilfred Hardy

Additional artwork by Ron Jobson

DERRYDALE BOOKS
New York/Avenel, New Jersey

CONTENTS

A SALAMANDER BOOK

First published by Salamander Books Ltd.,
129-137 York Way, London N7 9LG,
United Kingdom.

© Salamander Books Ltd., 1992

ISBN 0-517-06741-2

This 1992 edition published by Derrydale Books,
distributed by Outlet Book Company, Inc.,
40 Engelhard Avenue, Avenel, New Jersey 07001.

This book may not be sold outside the United
States of America or Canada.

Printed and bound in Belgium.

8 7 6 5 4 3 2 1

CREDITS

Artwork by: Wilfred Hardy and Ron Jobson
Written by: Robin Kerrod
Edited by: Jilly Glassborow
Typeset by: Bloomsbury Graphics, London
Color separation by: P & W Graphics,
Pte. Ltd., Singapore
Printed by: Proost International Book Production,
Turnhout, Belgium

INTRODUCTION

Motor racing is one of the most exciting sports
in the world. Drivers travel at speeds of over 200mph,
competing on narrow, twisting circuits against a mass
of other cars all trying to beat them. This action-packed
book introduces you to the thrilling world of the race car
driver, showing you how drivers learn their skills, prepare
for a race, and drive their cars to victory. We also look
at the many different types of race in which they compete.
Read on, and maybe one day it'll be you standing on
the rostrum to get your bottle of champagne!

A RACING START

Only the top drivers compete in world-famous races such as the Formula One Grand Prix or the Indianapolis 500. But even the best drivers began their careers by driving in more modest races in less powerful cars.

If you want to become a race car driver yourself, there is no reason why you can't start right now! Karting is the ideal race for beginners – you can compete from the age of eight upward. Simple karts can be built at home, with lawnmower engines

and no gears. But serious karters race in specially built superkarts, which look like miniature race cars.

From Karts to Cars

After several years karting, drivers can move on to proper car racing. This can be done in events organized by national motor clubs, usually for the same make of car. The most popular set of single-make races in the world is the Formula Ford.

Drivers can then move up to Formula Ford 2000 and 3000, Formula Three and Formula 3000. To be a Formula One driver, you must have completed a season in Formula 3000 or be national Formula Three Champion. Then you can be awarded your Super A licence. You are now ready to race in Formula One!

Driving in Formula Ford represents the big step up from karting to international racing. Formula Ford cars are powered by 1600cc Ford engines.

Speeding around a circuit, young karters cut their teeth in motor racing. Like all race car drivers they have their fair share of thrills and spills!

READY FOR ACTION

During the months and weeks before the racing season, manufacturers build and rebuild their cars to try and make them as fast and reliable as possible.

Formula One cars are sleek and beautiful machines. The driver sits in a tiny cockpit with the engine behind him. The engine, usually with 10 or 12 cylinders, has the pulling power of as many as 700 horses!

Because drivers travel so fast, there is a danger that their car will lift off the track and start to fly! To stop this happening, the car is fitted with "wings" front and rear which help to keep the car down.

Mechanics discuss their car's performance before a Grand Prix race (above), while the driver stands by in his race kit (right).

A few days before race day, the cars practice on the circuit to "qualify" (be chosen) for the event to come. In Formula One races only 26 cars are allowed – the 26 fastest cars in the qualifying sessions. The positions of the cars on the starting grid also depend on their speed in the qualifiers. The fastest goes into the front or pole, position.

Fireproof
Balaclava

Advertising
patches from
sponsor

Fireproof
gloves

Fireproof
helmet and
separate
visor

Fireproof
overalls

Fireproof
boots

Formula One cars crowd together as they power away from the starting grid at the beginning of the 1991 Belgian Grand Prix. Note the blue haze from their exhausts.

Warming Up and Lining Up

On race day itself, the cars leave the pits, (service area) and move onto the circuit. First, they do a warm-up lap to warm up the engine. This also allows the tires to warm up; when the tires are warm, the rubber can grip better.

After the warm-up lap, all the cars line up in their pre-arranged positions. The drivers tense themselves as they stare at the starting lights. The red light comes on. The drivers rev their engines, making a deafening noise. A few seconds later the lights turn green. Hands select gears, feet stamp on throttles, and the race is on!

Cars race at high speed past the grandstand, and spectators cheer their favorite drivers until they are hoarse. Inside his cockpit, a driver steels himself for the moment when he can overtake the cars in front.

A DRIVER'S EYE VIEW

The fastest part of a Grand Prix circuit is the "straight," which is usually flanked by grandstand and pit areas. The spectators cheer noisily as the cars race past at frightening speed. But the driver doesn't hear them. In his cramped cockpit he is deafened by the noise of engines and exhausts, and by the rushing of the wind. He concentrates grimly on trying to find a way past the cars in front. He must also avoid being passed by cars coming up behind.

Head-Up Displays

From time to time the driver glances down at his instruments to check the engine speed, fuel levels and oil pressure. He also checks the warning lights to see if there are any problems with his car. But every time he glances down, he loses concentration for a moment. So new helmets are being introduced with a "head-up display." In these helmets, essential information is displayed directly in front of the driver's eyes, so the driver doesn't have to look down for one second.

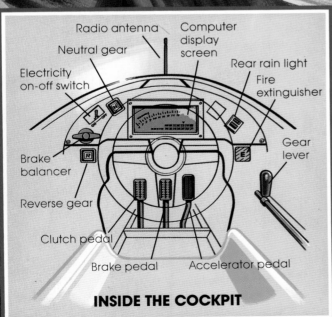

Radio antenna
Computer display screen
Neutral gear
Rear rain light
Electricity on-off switch
Fire extinguisher
Gear lever
Brake balancer
Reverse gear
Clutch pedal
Brake pedal
Accelerator pedal

INSIDE THE COCKPIT

SKILL ON THE CIRCUIT

During a race, a driver needs his wits about him all the time. His hands, feet, eyes and brain are constantly at work as he accelerates, changes gear and brakes his way around the circuit. He must have nerves of steel and lightning-quick reactions to take advantage in an instant when gaps appear ahead or when other drivers hesitate. In motor racing, he who hesitates is almost certainly going to lose!

The driver's main aims are to travel at the highest speed possible at each point on the circuit, and to cover the shortest distance. To do this he tries to follow a certain path, or "line." This is particularly important when cornering. If a driver is following the right line, he can take his foot off the accelerator and brake for the shortest possible time, so losing the least amount of speed.

Overtaking Skills

In most races, many of the cars are equally powerful, and can travel at similar speeds along the straights of a circuit. It is therefore difficult for drivers to overtake on the straights. But on the bends, it is a different matter. It is here that most overtaking takes place and the greater skills pay off. By taking a better line, "slipstreaming" or "outbraking" (braking late — see diagrams right) a driver may outdrive his opponents.

The leading driver has lightly touched his brakes and taken a perfect line into the corner. Now he begins accelerating again to regain his lost speed.

DRIVING THE LINE

Drivers try to follow a certain line as they travel through a corner. An ideal line is the one that slows them down least.

SLIPSTREAMING

The red car is traveling in the blue car's "slipsteam" (an area of low pressure behind a car). The slipstream gives the red car a "tow."

OUTBRAKING

By selecting a certain path through a corner, a driver can delay braking, and turning, until the last possible moment.

PIT STOP

When the race car driver is out on the track, he is not completely on his own. He keeps in contact with the rest of his team in the pits. As he races past the pits each lap, the pit crew supply the driver with details about his lap speed, his position in the race, and how far he is behind the leader. They do this by holding up a board giving him this information. They can also talk to him on the radio.

Into the Pits

In most races, the driver has to make a pit stop for one reason or another. He might return there to refuel or change tires, or because of mechanical problems with his engine, gears or brakes. Before he makes a pit stop, he radios ahead to make sure the mechanics are ready. He takes his car off the main track at high speed into the pit lane, where he pulls up in the position marked. If he is there for a wheel change, the crew move in with air-powered socket wrenches to free the wheel bolts. The wheels are replaced within seconds. Then the head mechanic signals and the driver speeds off to rejoin the race.

Above: In dry weather, race cars run on smooth tires. But, if the track gets wet, tires with treads must be fitted because these can grip in the wet.

During a pit stop, the pit crew work feverishly to change the wheels. The car is jacked up, the wheels removed and replaced, all in as little as six seconds!

PILE UP!

Motor racing is one of the most dangerous of all sports, with drivers trying to outdrive and outwit each other at frightening speeds on a narrow track. Cars are always designed with safety in mind (see diagram opposite). Dressed in his fireproof clothing, the driver is enclosed in a survival cell. This cell remains intact even in very bad crashes.

Many multiple pile-ups occur at the start of a race, when 20 or more cars hurtle neck and neck for the first bend. If a crash does occur then, the race may have to be stopped. It is restarted once the track has been cleared.

Further into the race, most crashes occur on bends. Sometimes a driver takes a bad line, brakes too hard or collides with another car. If he starts spinning, other cars may crash into him.

Raising the Alarm

As soon as a crash takes place, the alarm goes out. Track marshals race to the scene to help drivers out of their vehicles and fight any fires. Elsewhere along the circuit, other marshals wave yellow flags to warn drivers of danger ahead. If the crash is very bad, red flags are put out around the circuit to stop the race.

Roll bar protects head
if car rolls over

Safety harness

Crashproof
survival cell

Emergency
oxygen
supply

Cut-off
switch to
electrics
and fuel

SAFETY FEATURES

As one car swerves to avoid
another in its path, it is hit by a
third coming behind. In an instant
cars are spinning and wheels are
flying through the air. Soon there
is the added danger of fire. Yet
the drivers are so well protected
they can walk away unharmed.

Punching the air in triumph, the winner takes the checkered flag. He has battled against other drivers for more than 190 miles and came out on top.

THE CHECKERED FLAG

Of all the flags that drivers may see during a race, none is more welcome than the checkered flag. This signals the end of a punishing drive. For the first to cross the finishing line, the flag also means triumph. For the others, it means disappointment.

The winner returns to the pits with the cheers of the crowd ringing in his ears. The cheers swell to a roar as he climbs onto the winner's rostrum, where he is presented with a bottle of champagne.

Championship Points

Sixteen Formula One races take place in a season on circuits scattered around the world, from Europe, Japan and Australia to South America, Mexico and Canada.

The first six drivers to finish in each race are awarded championship points (10, 6, 4, 3, 2, 1 in order, from first to sixth place). At the end of the season, the driver with the most points becomes World Champion – the most sought-after honor in motor racing.

Right: Britain's Nigel Mansell takes the winner's rostrum after winning the 1992 Brazilian Grand Prix in a Williams-Renault. With him is team-mate Riccardo Patrese.

Indy cars scream around the banked corners of the oval circuit at speeds approaching 200mph. The track was once built of bricks and is nicknamed "The Brickyard."

THE INDY

Some of the fastest car racing in the world can be seen in the USA at the Indianapolis (Indy) 500. This race takes place in May on the famous Indianapolis Motor Speedway. The "500" refers to the length of the race – 500 miles. This amounts to 200 laps of the 2½-mile circuit.

Indy cars look much like Formula One cars, but have different kinds of engines. The engines run on methanol, a kind of alcohol, not gasoline, and are "turbocharged." A turbocharger is a kind of pump that forces extra air into the engine to make it more powerful.

Keeping a Constant Speed

Drivers hurtle their cars around the oval track at speeds up to 235mph. The corners of the track are banked (angled) so that the cars need not slow down much as they corner. This helps the drivers to keep a constant speed all around the circuit. Drivers try not to brake; they alter their speed by stepping on, or easing off, the throttle. And if they choose the correct line into and out of the corners, they need not alter the steering much. Every time they alter the steering, they lose speed.

RACING CIRCUITS

The Indianapolis Motor Speedway

The Monaco Grand Prix Circuit

Tunnel

The Indy is the best-known of the specially built oval circuits. Other race circuits have more twists and turns, like that at Monte Carlo on which the Monaco Grand Prix takes place.

NASCARS AND SPORTS CARS

Another famous oval race-track in the USA is the Daytona Speedway in Florida. It is the home of NASCAR, or stock-car racing. In the USA stock cars are production saloon cars that have been highly tuned and modified for racing. (In Europe a stock car is designed to battle and "bump" its way around the circuit.)

The two main NASCAR events are the Daytona 500 and the Firecracker 400. During these races, the drivers thunder their machines around the oval circuit at breathtaking speeds.

All Through the Night
A major event in the world of sports-car racing is also held at Daytona, the Daytona 24-hour race. Driver teams take it in turns to drive their specially built cars day and night over a longer circuit. But the most famous 24-hour race of all is the Vingt-Quatre Heures (twenty-four hours) race at Le Mans in France. At Le Mans, drivers compete at speeds up to 250mph over a distance of more than 3000 miles.

Drivers and their cars take enormous punishment during the race. Night is the worst time. The drivers have already been driving for hours and are getting weary. Things get even worse if the weather turns bad. Drizzle, a wet track and headlamp glare all combine to make the hours of darkness a living nightmare.

Above: Two NASCARS fight it out in the Daytona 500. Traveling at over 150mph, they are only inches apart! One has already been damaged in an earlier "shunt."

Left: This striking red and green Mazda 787B car won the 1991 Le Mans 24-hour race. Its three drivers took it in turns to drive the car in two-hour-long stints.

FAST AND FURIOUS

Perhaps the most exciting car races of all are also the shortest. They are drag races, in which two cars battle it out over a straight quarter-mile (440-yard) track. From start to finish, the race can take as little as five seconds.

This doesn't sound very exciting, but it is! The cars, called dragsters, are designed to accelerate very fast indeed. Specially built dragsters look like no other race car. They have a long, narrow hood and a huge engine behind the cockpit.

Space-Age Acceleration

When the driver steps on the throttle at the start of a drag race, his car shoots off like a rocket. The noise is ear-splitting. The driver feels himself pinned back in his seat with the G-forces astronauts experience when they take off.

In just a few seconds the car reaches 250mph or more and thunders over the finishing line. The fastest dragsters are fitted with a parachute to help them slow down quickly!

Below: With its exhaust pipes spitting flames, a powerful dragster blasts its way down the track. Like a jet aircraft, it is fitted with a tail fin to help keep it traveling straight.

Two dragsters thunder down the quarter-mile track, generating nearly as much noise and G-forces as a space rocket on lift-off. The fastest dragsters can reach a maximum speed of more than 290mph.

RALLY DRIVING

Rally driving is a tough, fast sport. Drivers need great skill and courage as they throw their cars around blind hairpin bends at high speed, or battle to keep them under control on muddy and icy roads. Their cars are specially prepared, with highly-tuned engines and strengthened bodies and suspension. Top rally cars now use four-wheel drive, with the engine driving all four wheels.

Most rallies are broken down into a number of stages. Some stages are run on public roads, others on rough forest or mountain tracks. At the start of a stage, drivers are sent off at intervals and race against the clock rather than each other.

Partners

Rally drivers depend heavily on their co-driver and navigator. Before the rally he or she prepares notes, called pacenotes, covering details of the route. During the rally, the co-driver yells instructions to the driver, telling him what the road is like ahead – for example, which way the road bends and how sharp the bends are.

Main picture: A rally driver hurtles his car along a rough desert track. At his side, his co-driver tells him exactly where to go so that he can concentrate just on driving. Both cars and drivers have to be tough to survive.

Left: Accidents happen often during a rally. That is why cars are specially strengthened. They are fitted with roll bars which help to protect the drivers from serious injury.

USEFUL TERMS

Note: Words printed in capital letters have separate entries.

Banger racing Circuit racing using bangers, or old battered cars.

Banking Building up a track at an angle. Corners may be banked on racing circuits so that cars can take them at higher speeds.

Black flag Shown together with a number on a signal board, a black flag informs the driver of that numbered car to return immediately to the pits, usually because he has broken one of the race rules. A black flag with an orange disc and accompanying board warns the numbered driver that he must return to the pits because of a car problem that could be dangerous. A flag with black and white diagonals warns a driver about his unsportsmanlike behaviour.

Blue flag This warns a driver that he is about to be overtaken.

CC Cubic centimetres. The engine capacity (volume in the cylinders) of race cars is expressed in ccs.

Checkered flag The black-and-white flag waved at the finish line to signal the end of a motor race.

Drag racing Racing over a quarter-mile (440-yard) straight track, with drivers competing in pairs. The specialist cars, called dragsters, are designed to produce the fastest acceleration possible.

Formula The class in which a race car runs.

Formula One The top level international formula in motor racing, for non-turbo cars with an engine capacity up to 3500cc.

Formula Ford One of the most popular motor-racing classes, for cars powered by 1600cc Ford engines.

G-forces The extra forces exerted on a driver's body when he accelerates rapidly or turns corners sharply.

Go-kart See KART

Grid (or starting grid) Lines drawn on the track that show the starting positions of the cars.

Grand Prix Literally "Big Prize," an international motor race for FORMULA cars.

Head-up display (HUD) A recently introduced device to display essential data in front of the driver's eyes when racing.

Indy car A race car like that used in the Indianapolis 500 race. Indy cars are raced on circuits throughout the USA.

Kart (or go-kart) A small, often open, race car with a small engine. It may be with or without gears.

Le Mans See Vingt-Quatre Heures du Mans.

Line The path a driver takes around a circuit.

Marshals Trained officials, usually volunteers, who are positioned around a circuit to assist in the running of a motor race. They display warning flags to signal drivers of hazards ahead, and they are on hand, with fire-fighting equipment, to help drivers in trouble.

NASCAR The National Association for Stock Car Automobile Racing of the USA. The cars that race under its rules are often called NASCARs.

Oval racing Racing that takes place on a specially prepared oval track. BANGER and STOCK-CAR racing take place on oval circuits.

Pits The service area along a circuit, where cars go to refuel, have their tires changed, or be repaired.

Pole position The front position on the grid for the start of a motor race.

Rally A motor sport in which two-person teams (driver and co-driver/navigator) compete with one another against the clock over a number of sections, or stages. These may take place on public roads and/or private off-the-road tracks. Big international rallies such as the Monte Carlo in Europe, the Safari Rally in East Africa, the Lombard/RAC Rally in Britain and Rally Australia in Australia take place over several punishing days. They are among 14 international rallies around the world in which drivers battle to become World Rally Champions.

Red flag Displayed around the circuit, a red flag means the race is stopped.

Revs Short for revolutions, meaning engine revolutions (turns). The speed of an engine is expressed in revs per minute, or rpm.

Slicks The smooth, treadless tires race cars use for maximum "grip" in dry weather. In the wet, tires with treads must be used instead.

Slipstream The area of low air pressure behind a moving car. A following car may enter this area and get a "tow" – this is called slipstreaming.

Stage A section in a car RALLY.

Stock car Has different meanings in Europe and the USA. In Europe it refers to strengthened vehicles that battle and bump one another around a circuit. In the USA stock cars are large powerful saloons that take part in ordinary (that is, no bumping!) races around banked circuits.

Survival cell The strengthened cockpit of a race car that helps protect drivers if they crash.

Turbocharger A pump, driven by a turbine, which forces extra air into an engine to increase its power.

Vingt-Quatre Heures du Mans The most famous 24-hour race for special sports cars. It takes place each year at Le Mans, a town in northern France, west of Paris.

White flag Warns drivers there is a slow-moving vehicle on the track in front, either a service vehicle or another car in trouble.

Wings Shaped fins fitted to the front and rear of race cars to help keep them down on the track. They are also called spoilers and foils.

Yellow flag When waved by a MARSHAL it means danger ahead. Drivers must slow down and not overtake until they see a green flag. A yellow flag with red stripes means a slippery track ahead.

WHAT TO DO, WHERE TO GO?

After reading this book you may imagine yourself driving a Grand Prix car to victory and winning the Driver's World Championship. This is a great ambition, but it will take you a while to achieve it!

But there are plenty of ways in which you can become involved in motor sport, and from an early age. As mentioned at the beginning of the book, you can take up kart racing at the age of eight or even earlier. And many children pick up their interest in motor sport from their parents, who belong to motor clubs and race cars themselves.

Shockers and Diffs
There are numerous motor clubs in most countries. Most concentrate on a particular make of car, such as the Mustang in the USA and the MG in Britain. These are two examples of what are called classic cars, ones with a long and interesting history.

Every club enthusiast will be more than happy to tell you at length about his or her particular make of car, talking about horsepower, ccs, crash gears, trailing arms, shockers and dampers, torque, diffs and propshafts: it's like a different language!

Look It Up
Motor racing in all its forms is so popular throughout the world that there are plenty of ways to find out more about it. Many clubs publish their own magazines, and there are plenty of weekly or monthly magazines on the news-stands, such as *Autoweek* in the USA, *Autosport* in Britain and *Chequered Flag* in Australia. Also, most television companies include motor racing among their regular broadcasts.

But there is nothing like experiencing the atmosphere of motor racing live. The high-pitched whine of high-revving engines, the ear-splitting roar of unmuffled exhausts, the smell of burning rubber, the roar of the excited crowd all combine to make motor racing one of the greatest of all spectator sports. Once you become bitten by the motor-racing bug, you are hooked for life!

There are more than 80 first-class circuits scattered throughout the world. The FIA (Fédération Internationale de l'Automobile) Formula One World Championship is held on 16 of them every year, typically in Australia, Brazil, Belgium, Britain, Canada, France, Germany, Hungary, Italy, Japan, Portugal, San Marino, South Africa, Spain, Mexico and Monaco.

Learn to Race
When you get older and maybe start racing in club events, you may want to learn the finer points of race-car driving. There are specialist motor-race driving schools in many countries. In the USA, for example, the Sports Car Club of America (SCCA) runs the National Racing School at Englewood in Colorado, and has schools in many other parts of the country too. In Britain, there are race car driver schools at several major circuits, including Brands Hatch, near Dartford, Kent and Silverstone, near Towcester, Northamptonshire.